I0821034

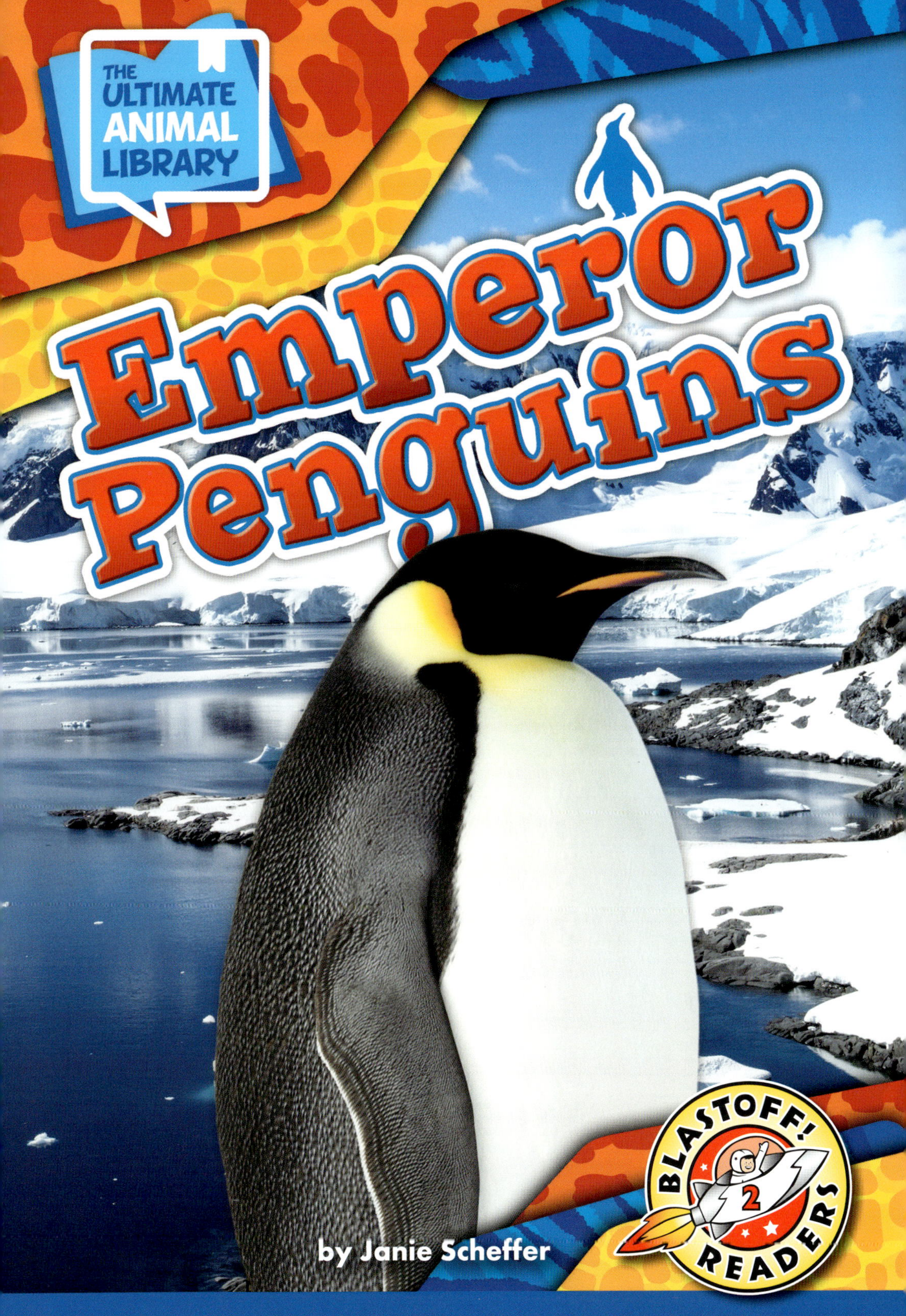

Emperor Penguins

by Janie Scheffer

BLASTOFF! READERS, AN IMPRINT OF BELLWETHER MEDIA BY FLUTTERBEE

Blastoff! Readers are carefully developed by literacy experts to build reading stamina and move students toward fluency by combining standards-based content with developmentally appropriate text.

Level 1 provides the most support through repetition of high-frequency words, light text, predictable sentence patterns, and strong visual support.

Level 2 offers early readers a bit more challenge through varied sentences, increased text load, and text-supportive special features.

Level 3 advances early-fluent readers toward fluency through increased text load, less reliance on photos, advancing concepts, longer sentences, and more complex special features.

★ **Blastoff! Universe**

Reading Level

Grade K

Grades 1–3

Grade 4

This edition first published in 2026 by Bellwether Media, Inc.

For information regarding permission, write to Bellwether Media, Inc., Attention: Permissions Department, 3500 American Blvd W, Suite 150, Bloomington, MN 55431.

Library of Congress Cataloging-in-Publication Data is available at www.loc.gov or upon request from the publisher.

ISBN: 9798893047936 (hardcover)
ISBN: 9798893048933 (ebook)

Editor: Elizabeth Neuenfeldt   Designer: Brittany McIntosh

Printed in the United States of America, North Mankato, MN.

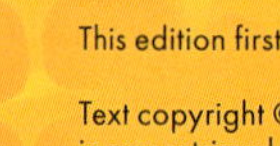

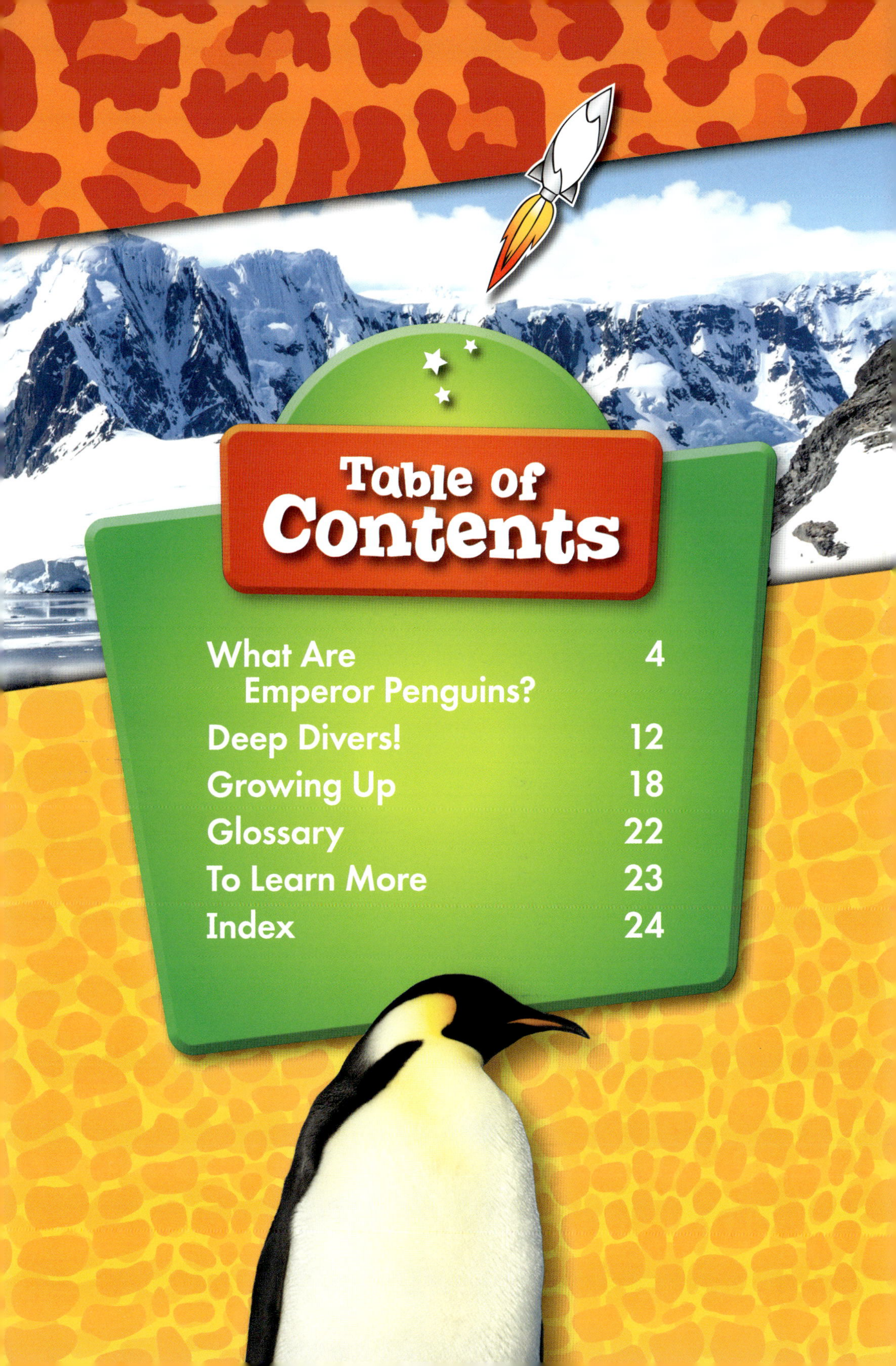

Table of Contents

What Are Emperor Penguins? 4

Deep Divers! 12

Growing Up 18

Glossary 22

To Learn More 23

Index 24

What Are Emperor Penguins?

Emperor penguins are flightless birds. They live in **Antarctica**. They are the world's largest penguins. They can be 51 inches (130 centimeters) tall!

Emperor Penguin Report

Range

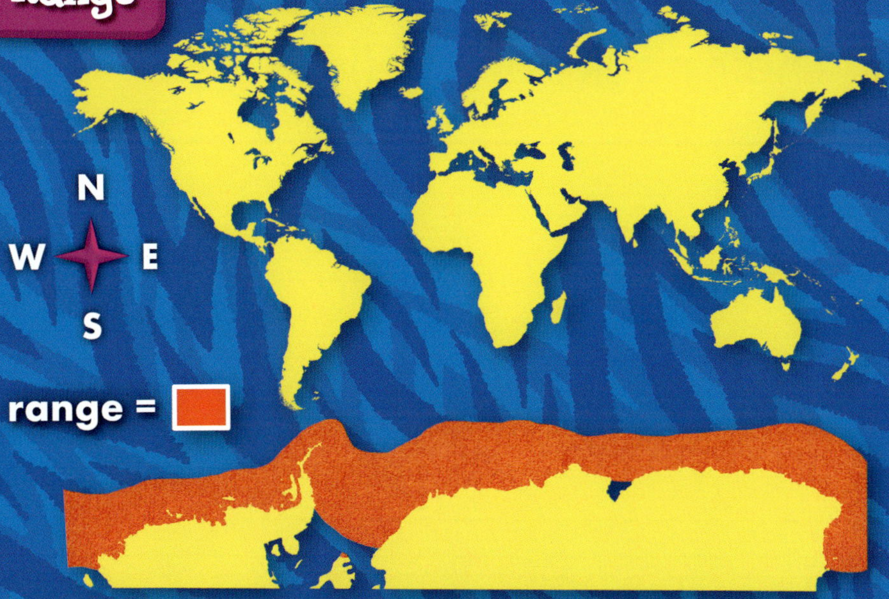

N
W E
S

range = ■

Status in the Wild

near threatened

Habitats

ice shelves

Southern Ocean

These penguins have black heads and backs. Their necks are yellow.

Their bellies are white. Their colors help them hide underwater.

Emperor penguins have layers of feathers. They stay warm!

They have fat on their feet. This keeps their feet warm on the ice.

Emperor penguins have **flippers** and **webbed feet**. These help penguins swim!

Strong claws help them stand on the ice.

claws

Spot an Emperor Penguin

Deep Divers!

colony

Emperor penguins live in big **colonies** on **ice shelves**. Some colonies have thousands of penguins!

Colonies keep these penguins safe and warm.

Emperor penguins are fast swimmers. They can quickly jump out of the water.

leopard seal

This keeps them safe from **predators** such as leopard seals.

These penguins dive deeper than any other bird. They can be underwater for more than 20 minutes!

Emperor Penguin Food Web

leopard seals

orcas

fish

krill

They dive underwater to hunt.
They are **carnivores**.
They mostly eat fish and krill.

Growing Up

Female emperor penguins lay one egg each winter. Males keep the eggs warm inside their **brood pouches** while females hunt.

The eggs **hatch** two months later. **Chicks** come out.

chicks

brood
pouch

Chicks soon join **crèches**. They stay safe while their parents find food for them.

Chicks leave their parents after five months. These swimmers live up to 20 years!

Life of an Emperor Penguin

Name of Babies

chicks

Number of Eggs

1

Time Spent with Parents

5 months

Life Span

up to 20 years

Glossary

Antarctica—the cold region around the South Pole

brood pouches—warm layers of skin where emperor penguins keep their eggs

carnivores—animals that eat only meat

chicks—baby emperor penguins

colonies—groups of emperor penguins

crèches—groups of young penguins gathered together to stay safe and warm

flippers—wide, flat body parts that are used for swimming

hatch—to break open

ice shelves—floating sheets of thick ice attached to land

predators—animals that hunt other animals for food

webbed feet—feet with thin skin that connects the toes

To Learn More

AT THE LIBRARY

Amstutz, Lisa. *Emperor Penguins: A Migration Story.* Mankato, Minn.: Amicus Illustrated, 2026.

Lock, Deborah. *Emperor Penguins.* New York, N.Y.: DK, 2023.

Owen, Ruth. *Emperor Penguins.* Minneapolis, Minn.: Ruby Tuesday Books, 2025.

ON THE WEB

FACTSURFER

Factsurfer.com gives you a safe, fun way to find more information.

1. Go to www.factsurfer.com.
2. Enter "emperor penguins" into the search box and click 🔍.
3. Select your book cover to see a list of related content.

Index

carnivores, 17
chicks, 18, 20, 21
claws, 10, 11
colonies, 12, 13
dive, 16, 17
eggs, 18, 21
feathers, 8
feet, 9, 10
flippers, 10, 11
hunt, 17, 18
ice, 9, 10, 12
predators, 15

The images in this book are reproduced through the courtesy of: Designpics, front cover (penguins); Nancy Pauwels, front cover (background), pp. 2-3; vladsilver, pp. 3, 18, 20, 21; Jan Martin Will, pp. 4, 11; AGAMI Photo Agency/ Alamy Stock Photo, p. 6; Mario_Hoppmann, p. 7; Andrew Peacock, pp. 8, 13; Vladimir Protasov2323, p. 9; Verbatim Vulgar Virtues 1, p. 10; Kevin Schafer/ Alamy Stock Photo, pp. 10-11; imageBROKER.com/ Alamy Stock Photo, p. 12; Nature Picture Library/ Alamy Stock Photo, p. 14; Angela N Perryman, p. 15; Bluegreen Pictures/ Alamy Stock Photo, pp. 16-17; Tarpan, p. 17 (leopard seals); Tory Kallman, p. 17 (orcas); Risto Raunio, p. 17 (penguin); Frederique Olivier/ Nature Picture Library, p. 17 (fish); SeaTops/ Alamy Stock Photo, p. 17 (krill); polarman, pp. 18-19; MrAli00, p. 23.